Men
to Avoid
in Art
and Life

Men
to Avoid
in Art
and Life

Nicole Tersigni
Foreword by Jen Kirkman

CHRONICLE BOOKS

SAN FRANCISCO

Library of Congress Cataloging-in-Publication Data:

Names: Tersigni, Nicole, author.
Title: Men to avoid in art and life / Nicole Tersigni.
Description: San Francisco : Chronicle Books, 2020.
Identifiers: LCCN 2020009294 | ISBN 9781797202839 (hardback)
Subjects: LCSH: Men—Humor. | Man-woman relationships—Humor. | Art—Humor.
Classification: LCC PN6231.M45 T47 2020 | DDC 817/.6—dc23
LC record available at https://lccn.loc.gov/2020009294

Manufactured in China.

Designed by Maggie Edelman.

10 9 8 7 6 5 4

Chronicle Books LLC
680 Second Street
San Francisco, California 94107
www.chroniclebooks.com

For Rob, who is the best kind of man.
For Zoe, who is already funnier than I am.
And for anyone who could use a laugh.

Foreword 8

The Mansplainer 10

The Concern Troll 28

The Comedian 44

The Sexpert 60

The Patronizer 76

Art Credits 92

Foreword

Hello,

You're about to experience a really funny book that—bonus—has gorgeous works of classic art. The title says it all if you're a woman: These are dudes to avoid in real life and in art. If you're a dude, you may be tensing up right now and wanting to put this book down and tweet at Nicole, "Not all men mansplain!" But then you'd be the guy who is mansplaining to a woman who ostensibly knows men, is related to men, has worked with men, is friends with men, that not all men are bad. She's probably come to this conclusion on her very own, and she trusted you to understand that she meant this "type" of man—one who still hasn't shaken off the subtle vice grip that the patriarchy has on his brain. If you think that Nicole doesn't know that not all men are mansplainers, you must think that she is stupid. Oh, by the way, Nicole isn't writing about herself in the third person. This is Jen Kirkman writing. I'm a comedian who is writing this part of the book called "the Foreword." (See how annoying it is to be 'splained?)

I spend my days online having my jokes explained back to me or, if I ask a rhetorical question, it's actually answered by men who explain something that I couldn't have even sarcastically asked if I didn't already know the answer to. It sounds like minutia, and it is, but it's maddening nonetheless. There are subtle ways that women are still micro-aggressed even by the coolest "I think that America is ready for a woman president" dudes out there.

Twitter is a daily reminder that I'm a woman. Twitter is trash. Let me be more descriptive, after all, this is a book and technically anyone contributing to a book should show that they have some writing skills. Twitter is a vintage store: It seems cool when you look in from the outside, but if you enter, you'll leave smelling like moth balls. Yet every once in a while, you find a gem amongst the heaps of discarded outdated things that make your skin itch, and this book is that. When I saw Nicole's Twitter thread showing examples of mansplaining in great art, I was able to laugh at this phenom that normally makes me want to jam a used tampon in my eye.

If you're holding this book because you're deciding whether or not to buy it—go ahead and buy it. Every sale brings a woman closer to her goal of dominating the publishing world; and if enough women do that, we could dominate the world. And once we do, we can explain things to men who didn't need things explained to them, and someday a man can write a book like this about women. Until then . . . laugh so hard reading this book that you get the attention of the guy in the cubicle next to you, or on the train next to you, and he can lean over and explain why this book is so goddamn funny.

And never forget that the great George Bernard Shaw once said, "If you want to tell people the truth, make them laugh, otherwise they'll kill you." The truth of what it's like to be a woman IRL and online is in this book.

Love,
Jen Kirkman

The

Mansplainer

"Let me explain your lived experience to you . . ."

"So now what you want to do is . . ."

"Yes, I know how to play Go Fish."

"Actually, I read that when you breastfeed, it's better for the baby if you lie down."

"...d that is my long and unsolicited opinion
...thing that is your area of expertise."

"... that's why it's actually harder to be a white man these days."

"I just wanted a refill."

"I know you play that instrument professionally,

and I don't,

but let me offer you some pointers . . ."

"I've seen you get water from this well every day, allow me to explain all the ways you're doing it wrong. Number one . . ."

"You might have a PhD in the subject, but according to this Wikipedia article I briefly perused . . ."

"I know being a stay-at-home mom is tiring, but if you prioritized your time better . . . "

"If you just ignore your menstrual cramps, they'll go away."

"All we're saying is we could, with no training or preparation, walk onto a tennis court and score a point against Serena Williams. Our penises would power our tennis racquets."

23

"Now, when you're riding a horse,

you need to make sure to keep a good grip on the reins."

"These are my horses."

24

"It's actually reverse sexism to hire a woman just because she's a woman.

Like, I could play that piano thing, too.

Probably."

The

Concern

Troll

"You should wear something less revealing if you want to be taken seriously."

"Listen, I would've given you that promotion. But I was concerned the extra responsibility would've been too stressful for you."

"When I said you should lose a couple pounds, I was only thinking of your health."

"I know you're upset about this issue,

but you'd get more people on your side if you didn't swear.

It's not ladylike."

"I think you should let me present your idea. You're so beautiful, it's distracting."

"Don't you think it's silly to get upset about how women are portrayed in media, when there are bigger problems in the world?"

"Someone is going to start saying you're a slut

if you sleep with too many people.

Not me. Someone else.

I think it's great that you sleep around.

I'm only worried about your reputation."

"Do you really need that doctor-prescribed medication?
I think it would really help your depression
if you just stopped being sad. Have some flowers."

39

"No one will take you seriously because of your baby face. Let me do the talking."

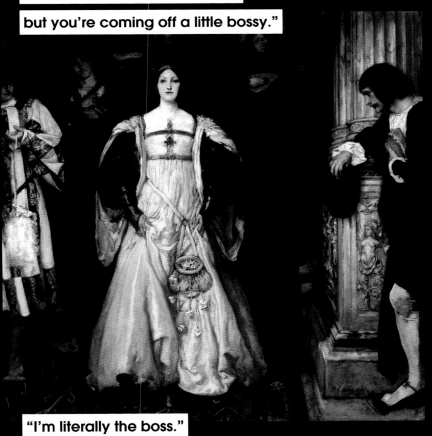

"I'm sure you don't realize this, but you're coming off a little bossy."

"I'm literally the boss."

The

Comedian

"Women just aren't as funny as men.

They've done actual studies on it.

It's not your fault, babe. It's biology."

"I was only kidding when I asked if those baby buffets had names.

You didn't have to call me a weasely little turd.

It hurt my feelings."

"You probably don't realize it,

but you just made a pretty decent joke."

"He's the greatest comedian of all time.

You just have to separate the art from the artist."

"If your dishwasher breaks just tell her to get back to work.

Get it? She is the dishwasher. You're not laughing."

"You didn't laugh at our very funny story.

Are you feeling okay?"

"If you have a problem with me whipping

my doodle-dasher out during your presentation,

"He said he wants you to touch his sack—
that's hilarious. Don't be so uptight."

"I don't think you understood my joke.

It's funny because the pigeon is dead.

He can't—you know what?

I'm just gonna tell it again.

Really listen this time."

". . . and women don't have to be funny

because men are already attracted to them.

That's why only ugly women

can tell a joke worth a damn.

Anyway, nice to meet you, I'm Bob."

"I was passing by and heard you say men can't take a joke, but you actually meant *some* men."

59

The

Sexpert

"I'm sorry, but I looked for your clitoris for a full six minutes.

I don't know what else you want from me."

"Let me explain something to you about the female body. . . "

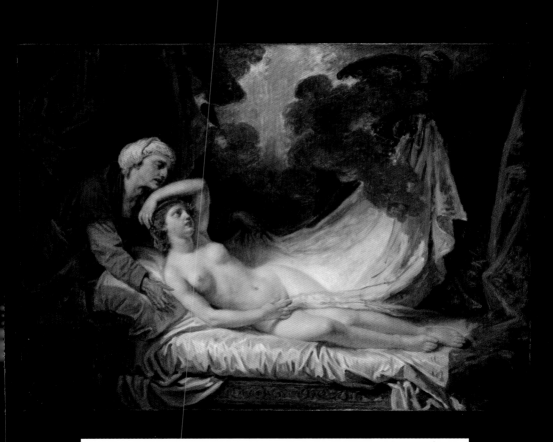

"But you can't be on your period. It's not a full moon."

"We've been over this a million times:

You can't get pregnant if you're on top.

It's called *gravity*."

"Please, please let me paint you nude.

All you'll have to do is sit there and smile.

And shave your bush,

because no one wants to see a woman with body hair.

It's unnatural."

"Here's a song I wrote called 'If You Can't Orgasm from Vaginal Penetration You're Probably a Lesbian, Linda'."

"So many women don't understand the essence of female sexuality."

69

"I told you foreplay is a myth. We didn't even need it."

"I know my butt smells like a hamster cage, but you need to wash your feet thoroughly before I touch you."

71

"You can't show that much skin
and expect me to not get aroused."

"I know women don't usually like porn,

but I thought you'd enjoy this picture of my face."

The

Patronizer

"I didn't know you read real literature.

I thought it was just romance novels."

"Maybe I should give my bill to the man of the house."

"Oh, you're a Tom Petty fan? Name five of his songs. And don't say 'Free Fallin'."

"I can't talk to you if you're going to get hysterical."

"Men and women are just different.

Men are naturally good with swords

and women are more suited for taking care of children.

So you should get the babies down from the ceiling."

"You're not like other girls."

"My music is pretty experimental, avant-garde kind of stuff. I don't think you'd get it."

"I know I made the mess,

but you're so much better at cleaning than I am."

"I know it's hard for women to sit quietly, but close your eyes and listen. You might learn something."

"…and the average woman's skull is only this big. Which is why, neurologically speaking, men are smarter than women."

"I think it's great that you don't care what you look like."

"All I said was you're smarter than you look. How is that insulting?"

Art Credits

Pg	Title	Artist	Location
11	Paar im Gesprach	Simon Gluclich	Wikimedia
12	The Card Party	Casper Netscher	The Metropolitan Museum of Art
13	The Holy Family with Shephards	Jacob Jordaens	The Metropolitan Museum of Art
14	At Mouquin's	William Glackens	The Art Institute of Chicago
15	Tavern Scene	David Teniers	The Hermitage Museum
16	A Woman Playing the Theorbo-Lute and a Cavalier	Gerard ter Borch	The Metropolitan Museum of Art
17	Christ and the Woman of Sumeria	Benedetto Lut	The Metropolitan Museum of Art
18	Domestic Scene	Anonymous	The Metropolitan Museum of Art
19	A Goldsmith in His Shop	Petrus Christus	The Metropolitan Museum of Art
20	A Gentleman in Adoration Before the Madonna	Givoanni Moroni	The National Gallery of Art
21	Portrait of a Couple	Anonymous	The Cleveland Museum of Art
22	Company in a Garden	Barend Graat	Rijksmuseum
23	Three Figures Dressed for a Masquerade	Louis-Joseph le Lorrain	The National Gallery of Art

24	**Lady and Gentleman on Horseback**	Aelbert Cuyp	The National Gallery of Art
25	**Philosophy and Christian Art**	Daniel Huntingon	Los Angeles Contemporary Museum of Art
27	**The Love Song**	Sir Edward Burne-Jones	The Metropolitan Museum of Art
29	**The Proposal**	Jan Steen	Private Collection
30	**A Young Woman and a Cavalier**	Cornelis Bisschop	The Metropolitan Museum of Art
31	**The Declaration of Love**	Jean Francois de Troy	The Metropolitan Museum of Art
32	**Antoine Laurent Lavoisier and His Wife**	Jacques Louis David	The Metropolitan Museum of Art
33	**A Woman and Two Men in an Arbor**	Pieter de Hooch	The Metropolitan Museum of Art
34	**A Man and a Woman in a Park**	Ludek Marold	The Art Institute of Chicago
35	**Alfred la Guigne**	Henri de Tolouse-Lautrec	The National Gallery of Art
36	**Behind the Scenes**	Jean Louis Forain	The National Gallery of Art
37	**Cymon and Iphigenia**	Benjamin West	Wikimedia
38	**The Irritating Gentleman**	Berthold Woltze	Wikimedia
39	**A Bridal Couple**	Anonymous	The Cleveland Museum of Art
40	**Moulin de la Galette**	Henri de Tolouse-Lautrec	The Art Institute of Chicago
41	**The Cascade**	Antoine Watteau	The Metropolitan Museum of Art
42	**The Hon. William Monson and his Wife**	Arthur William Davis	Los Angeles Contemporary Museum of Art

43	**Who is Silvia? What is She That All the Swains Commend Her?**	Adwin Abbey	The National Gallery of Art
45	**The Proposal**	William Bouguereau	The Metropolitan Museum of Art
46	**A Couple Drinking**	Jan Steen	Rijksmuseum
47	**Interior of an Inn with Figures**	Ferdinand de Braekeleer	Rijksmuseum
48	**Man and Woman at a Spinning Wheel**	Pieter Pietersz	Rijksmuseum
49	**A Man and a Woman**	Frans van Mieris	Rijksmuseum
50	**The French Comedians**	Antoine Watteau	The Metropolitan Museum of Art
51	**The Lovesick Maiden**	Jan Steen	The Metropolitan Museum of Art
52	**The Lovers**	William Powell Frith	The Art Institute of Chicago
53	**Sulking**	Edgar Degas	The Metropolitan Museum of Art
54	**Mooy-Aal and Her Suitors**	Claes Moyaert	Rijksmuseum
55	**The Poultry Man**	Ignace Brice	Rijksmuseum
56	**Double Portrait of a Young Couple as Granide and Diaphilo**	Yan Mijtens	Rijksmuseum
57	**The Petition**	Jean Louis Forain	The National Gallery of Art
58	**Paris Street; Rainy Day**	Gustave Caillebotte	The Art Institute of Chicago
59	**Portrait of a Woman with a Man at a Casement**	Filippo Lippi	The Metropolitan Museum of Art
61	**Clothing the Naked**	Michiel Sweerts	The Metropolitan Museum of Art

62	**A Confidential Chat**	Adriaen van Ostade	Rijksmuseum
63	**Aegina Visited by Jupiter**	Jean-Baptiste Greuze	The Metropolitan Museum of Art
64	**The Two Central Figures in Derby Day**	William Powell Frith	The Metropolitan Museum of Art
65	**Anunciation to the Virgin**	Jacob de Wit	Rijksmuseum
66	**Anthony van Dyk Wooing his Model**	Gustave Wappers	Rijksmuseum
67	**Bacchus and Ariadne**	Guido Reni	Los Angeles Contemporary Museum of Art
68	**The Lutenist**	Hendrick Martensz	Rijksmuseum
69	**Portrait of a Woman and a Man in an Interior**	Matthias Wulfraet	Rijksmuseum
70	**Mars and Venus Allegory of Peace**	Louis Jean Francois La Grenee	The Getty Museum
71	**Lady Undressing for a Bath**	Gerardus Duyckinck	The National Gallery of Art
72	**Susannah and the Elders**	Johann Carl Loth	The Getty Museum
73	**The Garter**	Jean Francois de Troy	The Metropolitan Museum of Art
74	**Before**	William Hogarth	The Getty Museum
75	**Portrait of a Woman and a Man**	Jan Willem Pieneman	Rijksmuseum
77	**Hendrick Arend van den Brink and his Wife Lucretia**	Louis Moritz	Rijksmuseum
78	**Henri Degas and his Niece Lucie Degas**	Edgar Degas	The Art Institute of Chicago

79	**Market Gossip**	Jean Henri de Coene	Rijksmuseum
80	**Morning Visit**	Adriaan de Lelie	Rijksmuseum
81	**Pear Making Music**	Cornelis de Man	Rijksmuseum
82	**Portrait of a Man and His Wife**	Ulrich Apt the Elder	The Metropolitan Museum of Art
83	**Portrait of Willem II and Mary Stuart**	Gerard van Honthorst	Rijksmuseum
84	**Sir Henry Capel**	Sir Peter Lely	The Metropolitan Museum of Art
85	**The Dance**	Aime Gabriel Adolphe Bourgoin	Rijksmuseum
86	**Unseemly Love**	Cornelis Troost	Rijksmuseum
87	**The Duet**	Charles van Beveren	Rijksmuseum
88	**The Drawing Lesson**	Louis Moritz	Rijksmuseum
89	**The Greek Lovers**	Henry Peters Gray	The Metropolitan Museum of Art
90	**Pieter Cnoll, Cornelia, and Their Daughters**	Jacob Coeman	Rijksmuseum
91	**Portrait of Robert Muys and his Wife**	Nicholaes Muys	Rijksmuseum